Angela Royston | **How to get ahead in**

IT & Administration

D1334025

www.raintreepublishers.co.uk

Visit our website to find out more information about **Raintree** books.

To order:

 Phone 44 (0) 1865 888113

 Send a fax to 44 (0) 1865 314091

 Visit the Raintree bookshop at **www.raintreepublishers.co.uk**
to browse our catalogue and order online.

First published in Great Britain by Raintree,
Halley Court, Jordan Hill, Oxford OX2 8EJ,
part of Harcourt Education.
Raintree is a registered trademark of
Harcourt Education Ltd.

© Harcourt Education Ltd 2007
First published in paperback in 2008
The moral right of the proprietor has
been asserted.

Editorial: Melanie Waldron, Lucy Beevor
and Kate Buckingham
Design: David Poole and Calcium
Picture Research: Ruth Blair
and Maria Joannou
Production: Huseyin Sami
Originated by Chroma Graphics
Printed and bound in China by
South China Printing Company

10 digit ISBN 1 406 20449 8 (hardback)
13 digit ISBN 978 1 4062 0449 0 (hardback)
11 10 09 08 07
10 9 8 7 6 5 4 3 2 1

10 digit ISBN 1 406 20461 7 (paperback)
13 digit ISBN 978 1 4062 0461 2 (paperback)
12 11 10 09 08
10 9 8 7 6 5 4 3 2 1

British Library Cataloguing in Publication Data
Royston, Angela
IT and Administration. – (How to get ahead in)
004'.02341
A full catalogue record for this book is available
from the British Library.

Acknowledgements
The publishers would like to thank the
following for permission to reproduce
photographs: Alamy Images pp. **31**
(John Walmsley), **20** (Kolvenbach), **11**
(Photofusion/Paula Solloway), **33** (Pictor
International); Angela Royston pp. **43**, **51**;
Corbis pp. **4** (Gerhard Steiner),
12 (Helen King), **19** (Jon Feingersh), **8** (Mario
Beauregard), **37** (Patrik Giardino), **35** (Richard
Klune), **16** (Ted Horowitz); Getty Images pp.
39, **50** (Iconica/Zia Soleil), **10**, **28**
(Photonica), **40** (Stone/Christopher Bissell),
27 (Stone/Mike Powell), **45** (Taxi/Philip Lee
Harvey), **43** (The Image Bank/White Packert),
13 (The Images Bank/Marc Romanelli);
Harcourt Education pp. **29**, **46** (Tudor
Photography); Magnum Pictures p.**25** (Peter
Marlow); Photos.com p.**7**; Report Digital pp.
15, **18** (John Harris), **49** (Paul Box);
Rex Features p.**17** (Philippe Hays);
Science Photo Library p.**23** (Dr Jurgen Scriba).

Cover photograph of X-ray image of a computer
mouse, reproduced with permission of Corbis.

The publishers would like to thank David
Clapham for his assistance in the preparation
of this book.

Contents

Words appearing in the text in bold, **like this**, are explained in the glossary.

What are IT and administration?

Do you enjoy working on computers or with computers? If so, a career in IT (information technology) or administration could be for you. Almost every office today has at least one computer. Computer systems and the Internet are playing a bigger and bigger role in companies and organizations such as hospitals, libraries, and Government departments. Computers and computer systems are all developed and set up by people who work in IT. However, if you like working on computers but are more interested in using them to help an organization run smoothly, you could think about a career in administration.

below: *Computers and administrators are important to all companies and offices.*

What is IT?

IT includes all the machines and systems that store or send information. It includes telephones, television and, of course, computers. Organizations store most of their information on computers and email is used to send and receive information. Computer manufacturers design, make, and sell computers. These and other companies provide help and advice to people when they have a problem with their machine.

Organizations do more than store information on computers. They develop special computer programs that help them run the business. Large organizations have departments of people who write these computer programs. They also employ IT staff to look after and repair the computers and computer systems when they go wrong.

What is administration?

Every organization employs people who work in administration. They include receptionists, secretaries, and all the people who look after office supplies, sort incoming mail, arrange meetings, and much more. They help to run the organization and every department in it.

Most large companies have two departments dealing with particular aspects of administration – finance and human resources. People in finance are responsible for all of the company's money, while human resources takes care of everything related to the staff, such as employing new staff and arranging training. Without good business administration, a company would soon fail. Even very small companies with just one or two employees usually employ someone whose main job is administration.

Get ahead!

There are so many different jobs in IT and administration that you should be able to find a job to apply for, whether you have very basic qualifications or a university degree. But the better your academic qualifications, the more jobs will be open to you and the better you will be paid. You can improve your qualifications by doing training courses in the area you are interested in.

Chapter 1

Right for you?

What does working in IT involve? It certainly involves computers, both the **hardware** and the **software**. Computers, printers, and all the machines connected to a computer are called computer hardware. The computer programs and **applications** that you use on your computer are the software. Telephones are essential to IT and television also plays a part. Computers, telephones, television, and radio can all be linked together through the Internet.

Hardware

You may have a personal computer at home on which you research and write homework, play music, and play computer games. Almost everyone in an office has a personal computer, although, of course, they should not use it to play music or games – unless they work for a games company! In an office, most of the computers are linked together to form a **network**. This means that they can easily share information and files.

Software

Each person's computer is loaded with the software they need for their jobs. Companies use many of the same applications as each other, for example for writing letters, making tables and **spreadsheets**, and paying salaries. Large or specialized companies probably also have software that has been specially designed for them. Special software may be used in only one part of the business. For example, the research department of an oil company uses special software to help detect new sources of oil deep below the ground. Other software may be used throughout the company. A travel agent, for example, will use the same program in all of its branches for booking holidays.

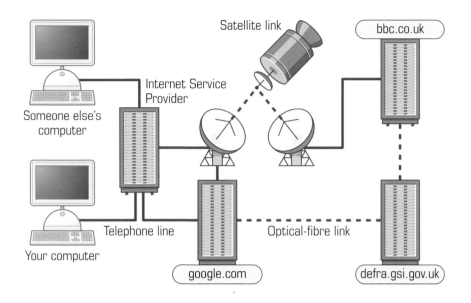

The Internet

The Internet is a network of very large computers, called servers, which store enormous amounts of information. The information is stored as millions of different websites that are created by individual people or companies. The diagram above shows how your computer can link to the Internet. Anyone can have a website and companies are using them more and more to advertise themselves and to sell their goods or services. The Internet is creating ever more jobs – working for service providers, designing websites, and handling business produced through the Internet.

Telecommunications

Most computers are networked using telephone lines, and access to the Internet and email is available through these lines. Mobile phones are mini computers. They send and receive signals, not through telephone lines but as signals transmitted like radio signals.

below: *Mobile phones are mini computers that can send and receive messages.*

Fanatical about computers?

To enjoy working in IT you need to be fascinated by computers and confident working with them. For many jobs you need to have a degree or a **BTEC** HNC/HND in Computer Science or Computer Studies, or a Mathematics or Engineering degree. It certainly helps if you are good at Maths and Science or Technology as well as having good IT skills. But do you also have the right personality?

Well organized and methodical?

For computer programs to work, all the instructions have to be exactly right and in the right order. For this reason, you need to be **logical** in the way you think and be prepared to work through a problem **methodically** – one step at a time. In many jobs in IT, you have to work under pressure so you have to be well organized, confident about your IT skills, and calm.

below: *Being good at mathematics is important for most careers in IT.*

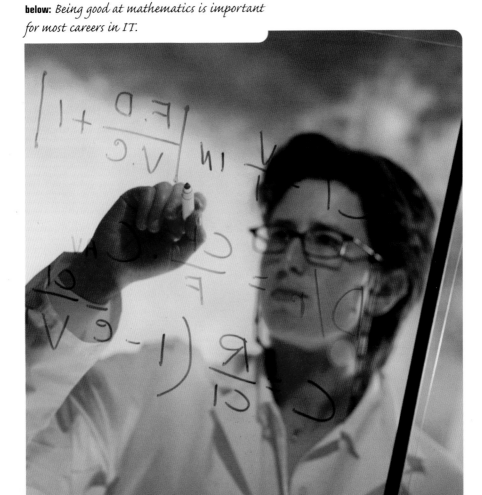

Problem-solver?

Do you enjoy logical games, such as chess and Go, or do you like Sudoku and crosswords? If you do, you may well be good at solving problems in IT. Sometimes it may be working out why a computer or a computer application keeps crashing, or it may be a problem that involves a whole computer network. If you are developing computer programs or systems, you will have to work out what is required and the best way to achieve it.

Good communicator?

You may be good at solving technical problems, but how good are you at explaining technical things to people who aren't? Many jobs in IT involve helping people with their computer problems, or training them in how to use a new application or computer system. It is easy to test yourself on this skill – just try explaining a recent development in mobile phones or computer technology to someone who knows little about it.

Finishing the job

Many jobs in IT involve working to deadlines. This means that a job has to be finished by a particular date, or even time. To achieve this, you may often have to stay late until the problem is solved or the task completed. Most people who work in IT enjoy their jobs and often choose to stay late to finish what they are doing.

Get ahead!

One thing you can be sure about in IT is that the technology is always changing. Keeping up to date with technological changes is important and something that you can do now. Read computer magazines, for example, and browse the websites of computer manufacturers and mobile phone companies.

Working in administration

Administration involves organizing people and the way they work. It can include directors, who run whole organizations, and managers, who run different departments. But it can also include many administrative assistants, who help to organize each department and keep it running smoothly. Finance departments and human resources departments are entirely involved with administration. Sometimes administration is the only purpose of an organization – the **Civil Service**, for example, is responsible for putting Government policies into action and running them.

Day-to-day administration

Most offices employ **clerical** assistants – clerks, secretaries, and receptionists. Their jobs include typing letters and reports, filing, ordering stationery, arranging meetings, sending faxes, and greeting visitors. Receptionists work for the whole company, but clerks and secretaries usually work within one department. Without efficient administration the department or company would soon grind to a halt!

Finance departments

Businesses have to make a profit. This means that they have to make more money than they spend. It is the job of finance departments to keep track of every payment the company makes and receives. Payments out include salaries and paying for goods and services, from postage and electricity bills to new equipment and tax.

Human resources

The greatest strength of many companies and organizations is their staff. It is the job of human resources (HR) to advertise jobs and hire new members of staff. They also provide training courses for staff or arrange for them to attend training courses outside the company. Training does not just help employees – having better trained staff helps the company too. A human resources department also looks after the staff's welfare. It may help with personal problems that arise in an employee's job or in relations with other employees.

Administrative organizations

The Government employs thousands of people in the Civil Service to administer their policies, from issuing driving licences to inspecting schools. Similarly local authorities employ people to run council services, such as collecting rubbish and giving planning permission for new building work. You can find out more about these organizations in Chapter 4.

CASE STUDY

Andy works as a medical receptionist.

I have just finished school and am working as a temp to earn money before going to university. At the moment I am working as a receptionist in a community health centre for drop-in patients. I answer the phone, get patients' notes ready, assist patients, and oversee the general tidiness of the reception area. Working for the temp agency is giving me lots of experience in admin jobs in different organizations.

below: *Being a good administrator involves getting on well with people and having a friendly manner.*

Are you suited to admin?

To work in administration you definitely have to be well organized and good at putting things into order. Can you set up a system for doing something and keep to it? You have to in admin! You also need to have a clear head and good understanding of the bigger picture – how the department or company works. There are so many jobs in admin at different levels that, whatever your academic qualifications, you will be able to find something that you are qualified for. Your personal and computer skills are, in many ways, more important.

left: *This administrative assistant is multitasking – carrying out more than one job at the same time.*

Computer skills

Much of the work in an office is done on computer, so it is important to have good computer skills. Information is exchanged by email, while letters, reports, and **minutes** of meetings are typed up on a computer. Files and important information are stored on computers. Many documents, however, are printed out and kept on paper – so accurate filing is also important.

What to do first

Most administrative jobs are made up of many different tasks and responsibilities. You have to be good at putting jobs in order of priority – that is, doing the most important ones first. And sometimes you have to be good at doing several things at once – multitasking!

Working in a team

In administration you are part of a team. In a small company or in a department, you work with other people to help them do their jobs. You need to be good at getting on with people. At times you will probably have to accept orders and at other times you will have to ask other people to do things, or to do things in a particular way. The administrative person is often called upon to help solve problems that arise, whether it is getting something into the post on time, arranging a last-minute meeting or rushing out to get lunch for a stressed colleague. You have to be prepared to turn your hand to almost anything.

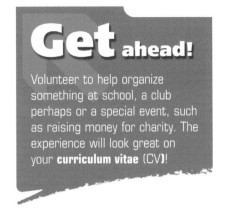

Get ahead!

Volunteer to help organize something at school, a club perhaps or a special event, such as raising money for charity. The experience will look great on your **curriculum vitae** (CV)!

Communication skills

All of this requires good communication skills. Can you listen and take in information accurately. Are you confident enough to ask questions when you don't understand something, and can you explain or relay information to other people? Are you **tactful** as well as **assertive**?

below: *Being able to take in and pass on information quickly and clearly is an important administrative skill.*

Work experience

When you are in Years 10 or 11, your school will either organize work experience for you or ask you to organize it yourself. Work experience is when you work for an organization for one or two weeks without being paid. It is an excellent opportunity to discover whether a particular line of work interests you. If you think you may be interested in IT or administration, this is your chance to find out! Reading this book will give you a good idea of the kind of organizations to approach for work experience in IT and administration.

What happens?

People on work experience are usually assigned to help a particular worker who will tell you what to do and show you how to do simple tasks. If you are working in an office you will probably have to do things such as photocopying, filing, and making tea and coffee. At the same time, you should be given experience of more demanding tasks so that you learn how the organization works and what people in it do. Your school will expect you to keep a log book, or diary, of what you do each day.

above: *You will learn a lot of new skills while on work experience.*

above: *These commuters are obviously expected to dress formally for work.*

Making a good impression

Make sure that you always arrive punctually for work. Dress smartly: notice what other people in the company wear and try to dress in the same way. Listen carefully when you are told what to do or how to do something. If there is anything you do not understand ask for more explanation, and do what you are asked to do willingly. If you do well on work experience the organization should give you a good reference (a report on the quality of your work). You will need references when you apply for courses or for jobs.

CONDITIONS OF WORK

The term "conditions of work" refers to pay, where you work, hours of work, and time off for holidays. Both IT and administration are, on the whole, office jobs and offices are usually open from 9 a.m. to 5 p.m., Monday to Friday. Conditions of work also include any extra benefits the company provides for their staff, such as a canteen where you can buy food cheaply. You may also be able to buy the things the company produces more cheaply. This is a bigger advantage if they make clothes or CDs, rather than nuts and bolts!

Get ahead!

Check out the website for the National Council for Work Experience: www.work-experience.org/ It tells you what to expect and helps you to prepare for work experience.

Chapter 2

Working in the IT world

Many different kinds of companies are directly involved in IT. They include companies who manufacture IT equipment, telephone companies, software producers, and Internet service providers. Some are huge companies that employ thousands of people in many different countries doing a huge range of different jobs. Others are small companies, employing only a few people and mostly specializing in a particular area.

Manufacturers

Many of the manufacturers of IT are world famous companies, including, for example, IBM who make computers, Hewlett Packard who make printers and scanners, and Nokia who manufacture mobile phones. If this interests you, you could be working in a fast-changing, highly technical industry.

Telecom companies

IT relies on information in the form of signals being passed almost instantly from one piece of equipment to another. Telecom companies provide the means of transmission. In Britain the largest telecom company is British Telecom (BT). It owns the landlines that it and other companies, such as Cable and Wireless and NTL, use as well as providing high-speed data link-ups.

below: *Making and testing computers is a highly technical job.*

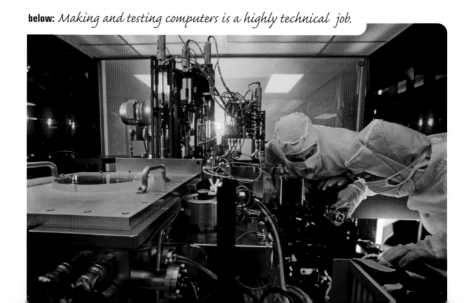

Mobile phone companies use microwaves and phone masts to send and receive signals, instead of wires or cables. Mobile phone technology is developing very quickly and mobile phone companies offer many of the same services as landline companies, such as sending and receiving text, pictures, access to the Internet, as well as phone calls. Britain's biggest mobile phone companies include Orange, Vodafone, and O_2.

above: *Many important developments in IT were developed in BT's research centre at Martelsham, near Ipswich in Suffolk.*

Software producers

Do the applications and computer programs appeal to you more than the equipment? If so, you should think about working on software. Computer companies and mobile phone companies develop software to run on their own equipment, while software houses develop applications for other companies to use. Some programs are designed and written for a particular organization. Hospitals, for example, use computer systems that have been specially designed for the National Health Service. Software houses also create general applications, such as a program for paying salaries and deducting tax, that companies can buy "off the shelf". Working for a software company means being able to analyse problems and situations and find solutions to fit them.

Internet service providers

Internet service providers (ISPs) are growing fast. They are the companies who connect your computer to the Internet and allow you to send emails. ISPs have huge computers that store vast amounts of information. They are connected to each other, so that you can access the whole of the Internet. Their customers use their ISP to communicate with other people, to research information, and to shop. People who work for ISPs constantly come up with new ideas and better ways of doing things.

Working on the hardware

Telephone companies and equipment manufacturers employ engineers, scientists, and technicians with all levels of qualifications. Engineers and scientists work in research, developing new systems. Engineers and technicians put the systems into operation.

Engineers and technicians

To be an engineer you need to be good at Maths and Science and to have a degree, BTEC HND, IT Practitioner Certificate or other qualification in Engineering or Computer Science. There are probably more different kinds of engineering than any other profession. Engineers who work in IT are mostly electrical and electronics engineers, and they work mainly with electrical circuits.

above: *This engineer has to have a good head for heights – he is climbing the phone mast to make a repair.*

The range of work is immense, from designing new microcircuits for computers to installing and maintaining **fibre-optic** cables capable of dealing with huge amounts of information. Computers and mobile phones have complex software built into them – that is how they work! Software engineers are constantly improving the software and designing new systems. They have to know about the hardware and the software.

Technicians are generally less well-qualified than engineers and are often specifically trained to do particular jobs. They may work alongside engineers or on their own.

above: *Help desk technicians give advice and technical help to customers by telephone.*

Help desk support

Companies that sell IT products and services almost always have a help desk. People who use IT equipment often have to learn how to use it and usually have no understanding of the engineering behind it. When they have a problem they ring the company's help desk. The person they speak to is an engineer or technician who is very familiar with the product and the problems that customers may have with it. They also have to be good at helping the customer to solve the problem by telling them exactly what to do. Help desk engineers need to be calm and patient, since customers are often confused and stressed.

Training

You can study for qualifications in Engineering and all levels of Computer Science at colleges and university. Whatever the level of your academic qualifications, you will be able to find a course that you can apply for. Look for courses that include work experience – there's nothing to beat learning on the job!

THE ARMED FORCES

The armed forces – the Army, Royal Air Force, and Royal Navy – all rely heavily on computers and IT systems and they will train you for free. You do, of course, have to be committed to joining the service, but, if you are, you will gain qualifications that are recognized by commercial companies when you leave the force.

Developing software

Software companies develop computer programs to help organizations run their businesses more efficiently. New software is developed by teams of people working at different levels. They include systems **analysts**, software developers, and computer programmers.

Systems analysts and software developers

Systems analysts, who are also called business analysts, look at the way a business works and suggests ways in which computer systems can improve it. Analysts have to have a good understanding of the particular business and the systems it already uses. They need to be up to date in computer developments and be able to come up with new and different solutions. They also have to be able to communicate their ideas to people who are not familiar with the technology.

Software developers work closely with systems analysts and clients to produce the software required. They have to understand the hardware the company uses and also be able to communicate with people who are not technical.

To be a systems analyst or a software developer you have to have a university degree or BTEC HNC/HND in relevant subjects, such as Computer Science, Information Management Systems, Business Information Systems or Software Development. Analysts usually have business training as well as computer qualifications.

below: *These software developers are testing software for a computer games company.*

Project managers

A project manager, also called a producer, is in charge of the whole project. They are the go-between between the clients and the software specialists. They have to make sure that the project is delivered on time and does not cost more than the budget.

Computer programmers

Computer programmers write the detailed programs to produce the software. They may use some existing programs and combine them with new instructions to fit the particular situation. They have to be very logical, methodical, and **meticulous**, since a single mistake may stop the whole program from working. Programmers also design what is shown on the computer screens so that clients can use the program.

Computer programmers have to be familiar with many different **computer languages** and have a degree in Computer Engineering, Software Engineering, Physics or Mathematics.

CASE STUDY

Teg is a computer programmer.

When I was at school I always enjoyed writing programs for my computer. My job now involves writing the programs for the computer games that you can play on **interactive** *TV. Recently, I reprogrammed the game Tetris for TV.*

I studied Mathematics, Computer Studies, and Physics at A level and then I did a 4-year degree in Engineering Science, during which I specialized in Computing and Robotics. My first job was turning Government documents into electronic format for websites.

Get ahead!

Java, C++, and PHP are among the most commonly used computer languages. Learning them will be a big asset if you want to become a computer programmer.

Working on the Internet

Websites are big business! Almost every company and organization has its own website and so do many individuals. Companies use their websites to advertise or sell their products or services and to inform people about what the company does and what jobs it offers. If this interests you, think about a career as a website developer, website designer, website manager, or graphic designer.

Website developers and designers

Website developers build new websites or improve existing websites. They work with clients to find out what they want from their website and help them to achieve it. They may work with huge **databases** – collections of information – and work out how to put them onto the Internet. Some websites are complex and, if they are selling goods, need to have a secure way for customers to pay.

Web designers find out what a client does and what they want their website to achieve. They design the separate screens that someone accessing the website will see and so have to make them as clear and usable as possible. They do the website programming and set up the systems for moving from one screen to another. Many websites include video clips, music, photographs, cartoons, and games as well as other interactive features.

Website managers and graphic designers

A website needs to be constantly updated and maintained. For example, special words have to be highlighted so that the website comes up when people search for subjects that relate to the website.

Graphic designers use computer software to create images, logos, and graphics that enhance the way the websites' screens look.

above: *This designer is creating a computer model of a porcupine fish.*

Qualifications

People with all sorts of backgrounds and trainings work on websites. Useful qualifications include a BTEC in Art and Design for **multimedia** or other qualification in Design and Multimedia. Look for courses in Web Design, Multimedia Design, and Interactive Computing. You need to be good at all aspects of websites – how they look and how they are used, as well as the programming that lies behind the site. You have to keep up to date with changing technology and software. Good business and **marketing** skills are useful as well as good IT skills, and an ability to talk to non-technical people about technical matters.

Get ahead!

Learn how to design a basic website. Type "build a website" into your search engine to get a choice of ways for designing your own website. Once you have the know-how, why not offer to design websites for your friends and family? The more experience you can build up, the more impressed future employers will be.

Chapter 3

Working with IT everywhere!

You don't have to work for a computer company to work in IT. All companies and organizations rely more and more on IT to help them carry out their business and run more efficiently. Smaller companies often use outside **consultants** to set up and maintain their computer systems, but larger companies and organizations have their own IT departments.

IT departments

Large companies have well-established IT departments that are responsible for everything to do with computers and IT in the company. They employ systems analysts, programmers, and people doing similar jobs to those in software companies. They design and **adapt** software to make the company work more efficiently. Large companies look for people who are not only well skilled in IT but who can come up with new ways of solving problems and who can communicate well, especially with non-technical staff. The IT department also maintains the company's hardware and keeps it up to date.

The table below shows a few of Britain's largest companies, which all have their own IT departments.

Company	What it does
GlaxoSmithKline	Makes pharmaceutical products such as toothpaste, painkillers, and other medicines
ICI	Makes paints, glues, food flavours, sunscreen creams, and other chemicals
Shell	Oil company producing petrol, and other motor oils
Tesco	The largest chain of supermarkets in Britain
British Aerospace	Produces aircraft and defence systems
Unilever	Owns many well-known companies including Birds Eye, Wall's, and Lever Brothers

above: *These people are working in a busy IT department.*

Computer consultants

Smaller companies that cannot afford to have their own IT department employ computer consultants instead. Computer consultants vary from those that offer services in developing particular software for companies to people who work on their own, giving advice and help to anyone who wants it.

Working on the Internet

Companies use the Internet to inform people about what they do, to advertise and sell their products, and often to advertise job vacancies as well. (It is well worth browsing the websites of well-known companies or companies where you live to see what they do and what sort of jobs they offer.) The websites themselves, of course, have been set up and are run by IT specialists.

Some companies, such as the search engine Google and the auction site eBay, exist only because of the Internet. Amazon and Play are just two Internet companies that sell books, CDs, DVDs, and other goods. Other companies use the Internet as well as more conventional outlets like shops. Every major supermarket and many high street shops have a website where you can order and pay for goods which the company then delivers to your home. You can also book holidays, rail tickets, and theatre tickets online. In fact there is very little that you cannot do online!

Working in an IT department

Some of the people who work in an IT department have the same skills as those who work for computer manufacturers, mobile phone companies, and other computer companies. In an IT department, systems analysts and computer programmers develop specialized software for the company. Software engineers make sure that the new software runs well on the existing computers and fits in with existing software. In addition, IT departments are likely to employ database developers, administrators, and network engineers.

Databases

A database is a bank of information. Many companies and organizations have large databases of people who use the organizations. Doctors, for example, store details of their patients on computer, charities store details of people who send them money, and companies store details of customers. Insurance companies keep personal information about each customer and details of what they are insuring.

A database administrator, or developer, creates the software for storing the particular information that a company needs. They work out how to organize the information and how to retrieve it – that is, they design what is shown on the computer screen so that people can easily use the database.

Data entry

Data entry clerks are the people who keep a database up to date and running smoothly. They feed new information into the computer and are particularly important when a new database is being created. They type in all the information that has, for example, been previously held as handwritten records. You do not need to have particular qualifications for data entry, but good mathematics and English language skills are useful as well as IT qualifications, such as the European Computer Driving Licence (see "Get ahead" on page 41). Market research companies and some Government departments are just two kinds of organization that employ permanent data entry clerks.

above: *IT staff may need to sort out problems with computer networks.*

Networks

Computers in an organization are networked so that each employee can access information and contact other employees by email. The network may link people in different buildings, even in different parts of the country or the world. Network engineers design the system and advise on the equipment that is needed by each employee. They set up passwords and all the other security required.

Some organizations have networks that involve clients or customers. For example, ATM machines are all networked by a particular bank. When you draw out money, the information is fed back to your account – all by computer! IT staff also maintain and run all the company's networks.

Computer support

Most computers are used by people who are non-technical. They know little about the hardware they are using, and even less about how the software works. Not surprisingly, when things go wrong they need help from someone who does. Some companies employ their own computer support staff to sort out problems and train staff in new systems. Other companies employ independent consultants to do the same job. IT equipment does go wrong, so repair technicians and service engineers are always in demand.

above: *As an IT Support worker, you will need to keep calm when your clients are not!*

IT support

Support technicians help employees with any technical problems that arise with the computer system. They have to be familiar with all the hardware and the software used by the company. They also have to be good at working under pressure and at keeping calm when dealing with frustrated employees. A major part of their job is teaching employees how to use the system correctly.

Computer services consultants

Independent consultants advise clients on every aspect of IT, from the model of computer they should buy to problems in operating the system. They help people over the phone or they go to their home or offices. Computer services consultants have to be very familiar with different makes and models of equipment and with the most common applications, such as Microsoft Word. Most of all they need to be able to communicate easily with people who have no technical knowledge.

Repairs and services

Equipment manufacturers and some computer shops employ technicians to repair broken computers. Some independent companies specialize in repairing faulty computers, while large companies employ their own technicians.

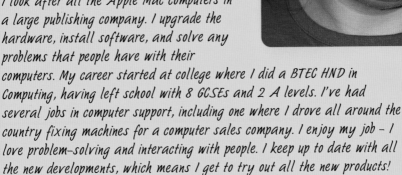

CASE STUDY

Amanda works in IT support.

I look after all the Apple Mac computers in a large publishing company. I upgrade the hardware, install software, and solve any problems that people have with their computers. My career started at college where I did a BTEC HND in Computing, having left school with 8 GCSEs and 2 A levels. I've had several jobs in computer support, including one where I drove all around the country fixing machines for a computer sales company. I enjoy my job – I love problem-solving and interacting with people. I keep up to date with all the new developments, which means I get to try out all the new products!

Get ahead!

You do not need particular academic qualifications for IT support or to train as a technician. BTEC, City and Guilds, and others offer an IT Practitioner Certificate which is useful for IT support, while experience in electronics or ICT systems helps if you want to train as a computer technician. Check out **apprenticeships** (see page 47), too.

Chapter 4

The world of administration

Although there are many kinds of organization, they all employ people whose job is administration. Whatever the organization the administrative jobs in them are very similar. Organizations include companies, the Civil Service, local government, hospitals, schools and universities, and non-governmental organizations (NGOs).

Companies

A company is a business that exists to make a profit for its owners, who are called shareholders. A private company may have just one or a few shareholders, while a **public company** has thousands of shareholders. The shareholders are not usually involved in the running of the company. That is done by the directors.

Larger companies are divided into departments that are each run by a manager with the help of administrative staff. Each department is responsible for a particular aspect of the business, such as buying supplies for a factory or sales. Managers may have a secretary as well as clerical assistants to help them run their department. Very large companies have a human resources department and a finance department (see pages 44–45) that help to run the whole company.

NGOs

NGOs are non-profit-making organizations that are independent of the Government. They include charities, such as Oxfam and Greenpeace, who collect money for a particular cause, professional organizations such as the British Medical Association and the British Computer Society, and other organizations whose purpose is not to make money. NGOs have human resources and finance departments just as companies do. Although NGOs do not make a profit, they have to work within the amount that they collect each year and every project is carefully costed and monitored. They also employ secretaries, receptionists, and other administrative staff.

Civil Service and local government

People who work for the Civil Service are called civil servants and their work is mainly administrative. They help to run the country by putting into action the decisions that the Government makes. Different Government departments deal with education, health, the environment, and so on. Some civil servants work directly with the public in, for example, social security offices and job centres.

Civil servants also work in local government. They are employed by local councils and each department is responsible for a particular service to the public, such as rubbish collection, schools, libraries, and parks.

below: *This secretary works in a school.*

Government and the Civil Service

The Civil Service runs **public services**, such as the National Health Service, social security, the armed forces, and the police. They also advise the Government on changes it should make to improve things and helps it to carry out those changes. Civil servants are paid by the Government from the taxes it collects from people and companies. Although the people who form the Government may change after an election, civil servants do not change with them.

Government departments

There are more than 150 different Government departments and agencies. Each one is responsible for a particular area of activity. The Treasury, for example, is responsible for the nation's money. It gives each department a budget – a fixed amount of money – to pay for everything it does. There are also many smaller departments, such as CADW, the department that looks after Wales's historic monuments.

The table below shows some Government departments and their main areas of responsibility.

Department	Responsible for
Health	the National Health Service, including hospitals, doctors, and dentists
Education and Skills	nursery education, schools, colleges, universities, and adult education
Environment, Food, and Rural Affairs	the environment, farming, fishing, and food
Foreign and Commonwealth Office	British interests abroad; works with the United Nations and other international organizations
Defence	the armed forces, police, prisons, and immigration
Passports and Records Agency	issuing passports and maintaining criminal records
Met Office	forecasting weather

above: *If you join the Civil Service, it is likely you will need some IT skills.*

Working in the Civil Service

Jobs in the Civil Service fall into one of three main areas. Many are involved in delivering services to the public, others do research and help to develop Government policies, while the third group work in human resources, IT support, and other areas that help the Civil Service run smoothly. The better your academic qualifications, the more responsible your job will be.

University graduates apply to join and, if selected, are then allocated a job afterwards. The work of the Civil Service is so wide that it does not matter what a person's degree is in – whether it is art, history or politics, there will be many jobs available to them. But you don't have to have a degree to join. All departments employ junior staff members who deal with customers, operate computer systems, update records, and help to run the department. The work itself varies enormously – you could be working in a minister's office, in a job centre or recording birth certificates.

EQUAL OPPORTUNITIES

The Civil Service has a strong equal opportunities policy, which means that everyone – women and men, whatever their race, religion or ethnic group – is treated equally.

Local government

Local councils are also called local authorities. They provide a wide range of services, from sports facilities and street lighting to the care of vulnerable and elderly people. Each local authority is responsible for a particular region and so is known as, for example, a county council, city council, borough council or district council. Altogether more than two million people work for local councils in Britain, so there are plenty of jobs and you'll be helping your local community!

Who runs local councils?

Local people elect councillors to run the local council. Councillors make all the main decisions and are unpaid, but receive allowances and expenses. The actual work is carried out by paid staff. Councillors often work in committees, who report back to the full council for important decisions. Some committees are open to the public, while others work behind the scenes, but all require a lot of administration in drawing up **agendas**, writing minutes, and sending them to everyone who needs a copy.

Councils receive money from central Government, from businesses who work in their area, and from people who live in their area and pay a charge called the council tax. Councils also make some money from, for example, parking fines and charges for swimming pools. Administering the money and keeping account of how it is spent provides many jobs. Communicating with the public is an essential part of local government work: informing local people about council services and dealing with queries and complaints.

Working for local authorities

Local councils employ people with all levels of academic qualifications, from school-leavers to graduates. Jobs are advertised in local papers and on the website www.lgjobs.com. They vary enormously. For example, if you are a school-leaver you may find a vacancy advertised for a museum assistant, a receptionist, a school secretary, or many others. Councils also employ graduates such as architects, town planners, and administrators.

The table on page 35 shows some local authority careers.

Area of work	Examples of careers for school-leavers and qualified people	Examples of careers for graduates
Buildings	joiner, electrician, CCTV operator, housing assistant	architect, building surveyor
Care	youth worker, home care assistant	residential social worker, policy development officer
Education and information	school secretary, teaching assistant	teacher, librarian
Emergency and environment	fire fighter, gardener, laboratory technician, dog warden	environmental health officer, civil engineer
Administration	elections officer, administrative officer, typist	accountant
Entertainment and leisure	pool attendant, museums assistant, leisure manager	archaeologist, sports facility manager

Get ahead!

If you are interested in local government, read your local newspaper and find out about your local council. What are the main local issues?

below: *Staff in council offices carry out a wide range of tasks.*

Working in administration

Chapter 5

If you are interested in working in administration, what sort of job should you look for? Working as a receptionist or a telephonist is a good place to start. As a receptionist or switchboard operator you learn all about the company or organization and how it is run. You learn about the different departments and the jobs people do. You also have a valuable job to do for the company. Receptionists and telephonists are often the first point of contact for members of the public. It is important that they give a good impression.

Companies, schools, doctor's practices, and almost all organizations employ receptionists and switchboard operators. In smaller companies, one person may do both jobs and many other things as well.

Receptionist

When you walk into a medical clinic or the offices of an organization, the first person you see is the receptionist. He or she sits at a desk near the main door and greets visitors and takes their details. They answer people's queries and may direct them to the right person or office. Receptionists may also take delivery of parcels and packages that are left for people in the organization. It is important that a receptionist looks smart and is friendly and welcoming.

Receptionists may have other duties too. They may answer the telephone, as a switchboard operator, and do clerical work such as photocopying, faxing, and typing. The receptionist keeps the reception area tidy and may order taxis for visitors.

Switchboard operator

Many organizations have just one or two main telephone numbers. Each employee has their own phone on their desk with their own extension number. When you ring the organization, the call may be answered by the switchboard operator, who then transfers the call to the right extension number.

Companies that receive many calls from the public, such as insurance companies or telephone companies, have automatic telephone systems. A recorded voice tells you to choose from various options to direct you to the department you need. Nevertheless there is usually an option to speak to an operator who will deal with your query.

Qualifications

You do not need to have any particular academic qualifications, although you can do a **National Vocational Qualification** (NVQ) in Reception or in Business and Administration. You need to be friendly, confident, and able to communicate well with the public.

left: *This receptionist is also the switchboard operator.*

Contact centres

Organizations that deal directly with the public usually have a contact centre, or call centre, to take orders and payments for products or services. Some contact centres concentrate on customer services – they answer customers' queries, advise them, and deal with their complaints. Insurance companies, travel companies, telephone companies, Royal Mail, the National Health Service, and companies that send out mail order catalogues, for example, all have contact centres.

If you enjoy talking to people on the phone and can keep calm and be patient when faced with frustrated or angry customers, this may be the job for you. You need to be able to speak clearly and understand a wide range of regional accents. Contact centre operators increasingly use email, SMS messaging, fax, and post as well as the telephone to communicate with customers.

Working in a contact centre

The work of contact centres varies but more and more companies use them to sell products and increase customer satisfaction. Contact centre operators work with a telephone headset, which leaves their hands free for the computer. They use the computer to access information or feed in information while talking to customers on the telephone. In an insurance company, for example, you are likely to be dealing with claims on insurance policies and feeding information about each claim into the computer.

In other contact centres, you might be dealing with a large range of information. In this case you would have to know a lot about the organization that you are representing. In a Royal Mail customer service centre, for example, you would give advice about posting letters and deal with complaints about lost or delayed post. In some customer service centres, the operator answers simple queries but passes more technical problems on to someone else.

Qualifications and training

You do not need to have particular qualifications to work in a contact centre, although a good education is useful. The main thing that employers look for is a good telephone voice and manner. Companies usually train contact centre operators themselves. They teach you the skills you need for the job. You may also sit with an experienced operator for a few days to find out how to handle different calls.

below: *Contact centre workers spend almost all their time speaking to clients on the telephone.*

Get ahead!

Contact centres take orders for goods and payments by credit or debit card, deal with complaints, and give advice about products or services. You may already have rung a contact centre, but, if not, you almost certainly will in the future! Note how the operator deals with your call, especially if you are making a complaint or you have a problem that needs to be solved.

Secretarial work

A secretary may work for the manager of a department or for the whole department. A secretary carries out much of the day-to-day administration, leaving the manager or the rest of the department free to concentrate on other work. Secretaries need to be well organized and calm. They have to communicate well and have good IT skills. Secretaries know almost as much as the person they work for and so must be able to be trusted with confidential (secret) information.

above: *Executives rely on secretaries to organise their day-to-day work.*

A director of a company usually has a personal assistant. The personal assistant has more responsibility than a secretary and may, in fact, be in charge of secretaries or typists.

Secretary

Secretaries work closely with their managers. They answer the telephone and make appointments for the manager, keep their diaries, and remind him or her when appointments are due. Secretaries need to be able to type and take **dictation**, either using **shorthand** or by typing from a dictation machine.

A secretary may arrange meetings for the manager or for the department. This may include booking a room and typing and distributing an agenda before the meeting. The secretary may then attend the meeting to take minutes.

Secretaries have many other duties, too. They open the post, for example, and make sure that their manager reads the most important letters and reports first. They may also file letters and documents. They greet visitors and are friendly and polite to them while they wait to see the manager.

Qualifications

You can become a secretary whether you have few qualifications or a university degree, but you do need to have some qualifications in English language and in computer skills. Most employers would look for secretarial training. The better your qualifications the more high-powered the secretarial job you are likely to get. People who have a university degree and secretarial training are often employed as personal assistants (PAs).

Specialist secretaries

Some secretaries specialize in medicine or law. Medical secretaries and legal secretaries understand medical or legal terms and the way, for example, that different legal documents have to be set out. Being bilingual (able to speak two or more languages fluently) is a great asset for a secretary. Look for a company or organization that has close links with the country whose language you speak and write.

Get ahead!

The European Computer Driving Licence is a qualification in computer skills that is recognized across Europe. It covers basic skills in using a computer, word processing, spreadsheets, databases, Internet, and email. You may be able to study for this while you are at school but, if not, you can search for your nearest centre on ecdl.co.uk.

Administrative officers and office managers

The Civil Service and local government employ thousands of administrative officers. Many administrative assistants provide secretarial support to their department and so their jobs are fairly similar. Some administrative assistants, however, have responsibilities of their own and their job is particular to the department they work in. Office managers have their own responsibilities too. Their job is to manage the clerical needs of a whole company.

Administrative assistants

An administrative assistant's job, like a secretary's, involves many different tasks. It may include dealing with mail – both emails and letters – photocopying, typing, filing, keeping diaries up to date, and arranging meetings. Many local government departments run services for the public, so administrative assistants in these departments may send out standard letters and forms and generally advise and help people who contact the department.

To be an administrative assistant you should have English, Mathematics and two other GCSEs (grades A–C) or S-grades (grades 1–3). You should also have a good telephone manner, be well organized and methodical, have good computer skills, and be able to work well in a team.

Office manager

Office managers usually work in smaller organizations. They are responsible for making sure that the office runs smoothly. They order new stationery, arrange for repairs and services for office equipment, and may be in charge of **petty cash**. They may deal with incoming and outgoing post as well. Offices cannot function without an office manager!

No particular qualifications are needed to be an office manager, but you do need experience. You need to know, for example, how all the office machines work and how to keep them running. You also have to know how every part of the organization functions. Office managers need to be well organized and able to prioritize.

left: *An office manager must make sure all the different aspects of the company fit together and run smoothly.*

CASE STUDY

Debbie is a corporate consultation and support officer.

I run a citizen's panel and a young people's panel for a district council. Different council services use the panels to get feedback about, for example, refuse (rubbish) collection and recycling or crime. I work with the service to draw up the questions, then I collate the responses and feed the information back to the service. I enjoy the variety in my job and being involved in the whole process. After leaving school with GCSEs I went to college and did A-level Business Studies and an NVQ in Administration. I joined the council as an administrative assistant, but before that I was a sales co-ordinator, marketing secretary and – my first job – an office junior. Having worked my way up, I've now got a job that really interests me!

Finance and human resources

Are you interested in keeping track of money? If so, a job in the finance division or accounts department might suit you. You won't be surprised to learn that you need to be good at mathematics and have good computer skills, too. If, however, you are more interested in people than in numbers and would like to look after the welfare of employees, then you could think about human resources.

Accounts

The finance division or accounts department looks after the organization's money. It is managed by qualified **accountants** but they are helped by accounts clerks with various responsibilities. Accounts clerks keep a record of every transaction – that is, of every payment that is made to the organization, and every payment that the organization makes to outside suppliers and to employees in the form of salaries.

One clerk may record sales in a sales ledger; another may file receipts and keep a record of purchases. A payroll clerk calculates how much money each employee should be paid, how much should be deducted for their tax and pension, and makes sure that they are paid on time. In smaller companies, an employee called a bookkeeper does all three jobs. The accounts department is also responsible for making sure that the organization pays all the correct taxes to the Government.

To work as an accounts clerk you need to have qualifications in Bookkeeping and Accounts from, for example, City and Guilds or the AAT (Association of Accounting Technicians).

Human resources

Human resources departments are run by a manager and human resource officers. They are graduates who have studied subjects such as psychology, human resource management, social administration or business studies. They advertise jobs that are vacant, select a short list of the most suitable applicants, and sort out the terms and conditions of employment for the successful candidate. Human resources officers may arrange training courses for new employees as well as conferences and further training for the existing staff.

above: *Some human resources departments organize team-building activities for staff.*

They deal with any problems that arise between employees or between an employee and their manager. They are often helped in their work by administrative assistants whose work will include typing reports, arranging appointments for interviews, booking conferences, and so on.

To work in human resources you must get on easily with people and communicate well. You must be tactful and able to make people feel at ease. You also need to be able to work in a team and have good English language qualifications as well as good secretarial skills.

Get ahead!

If you are interested in accounting and belong to a youth group or club, offer to help the treasurer look after the group's money. It is not as easy as you might think to get the books to balance!

Chapter 6

Getting in and getting on

Getting a job depends on three main factors: having the right qualifications, being the right sort of person, and presenting yourself in the right way. Getting the right qualifications starts at school. The subjects you take for GCSE/S-grades and Year 12 help to determine your future career. School subjects are often not enough, however. You usually need to do further education and training courses.

School courses

Many teenagers do not know what career they want to follow. In that case, the best subjects to take are the ones that most interest you and will give you a good, balanced education. If you do know that you would like to work in IT, however, you should definitely study Mathematics to as high a level as you can. Computer Science is also useful, provided it is fairly technical.

English Language, Mathematics, and IT are important subjects if you are interested in administration. Studying IT at school is a good way to acquire word processing skills and learn about databases, spread sheets, and so on.

right: *Colleges produce brochures like these, giving details about their courses.*

Training courses

Almost every college and university offers courses that are relevant to IT and administration, so how do you choose the right course for you? Probably the first thing is to think about what broad area you are most interested in. Think about which colleges or universities you would like to go to and then find out which courses match your entry qualifications.

Browsing the Internet, particularly the websites listed on pages 52–53, will give you lots of information. For example, if you are interested in IT, go to www.e-skills.com. The website www.learndirect.co.uk gives information about different jobs as well as courses all over the country. You can use it for all kinds of careers, including IT and administration. You can also type in the college you are interested in to find out about all the courses they offer and how to apply.

Work experience

Work experience is invaluable (see pages 14–15). It helps you to decide whether you are interested in an area of work. It gives you practical experience with which to impress colleges and future employers. Work experience is an important part of many courses, but why wait? The more experience of working you have the better. Never mind that you are not paid for work experience. It's a great investment in your future!

APPRENTICESHIPS

Would you like to be paid while you train? If so, then you may be able to do an apprenticeship in your chosen career. To find out more about what apprenticeships are available, go to www.apprenticeships.org.uk.

Application forms

Whether you are applying for a course or for a job you will need to fill out an application form. Before you get a job you will certainly have an interview. Both the application form and an interview are opportunities to present yourself at your best.

The application form is the first impression that an admissions tutor at a college or an employer will have of you, so make sure that you fill it in correctly and neatly. Check to see whether you are asked to fill it in block capitals and whether you have to use a black pen. Many application forms are photocopied and blue does not show up well. It is a good idea to photocopy the form several times and practise filling it in. Make sure you do not miss any questions. Only fill in the real form when you are satisfied that all your answers are the best possible.

Personal statements

Many application forms ask for a personal statement or reasons why you are applying. This is your chance to be really positive about yourself and catch the tutor or employer's attention. Before you begin, think about why you are applying for the course or the job. Make a note of all the positive reasons you have for doing it and any experience that you already have that is relevant. Think about your personality and how it is suited for the subject or job.

If you are applying for a course, you could include the career you hope it will lead to. It is a good idea to include something you have already done or read that shows your interest and commitment. Make sure that your personal statement is **grammatical** and that all the spellings are correct. If you can, type it out and attach it to the form. If you have to write in a space, make sure that your writing is large and clear enough to read easily. Do your best to make everything you want to say relevant to the form – and don't include things that are totally irrelevant.

above: *There are many ways of getting advice about careers – see the websites listed on page 52 for some of them.*

FINDING A JOB

More and more jobs are advertised on the Internet. Civil Service jobs are advertised on the Civil Service website and local government jobs are advertised on www.lgjobs.com. Check the websites of corporations and companies, such as Shell or Marks & Spencer, to see what jobs they are advertising. You can also check your local paper, and, for example, specialized IT magazines.

Interviews

If you are invited for a job interview, you are already doing well. An interview is your chance to find out more about the job and to convince the employer that you are just the person they are looking for. To do well in an interview you need to prepare thoroughly and present yourself well.

Prepare in advance

Find out all you can about the organization. Research on the Internet to find out exactly what it does and what its aims are. Charities have very clear aims and principles, but companies may also have mission statements. Agreeing with the aims of an organization is not enough, however. You should also find out as much as you can about the actual job. As with your personal statement, think of everything you have done that is relevant to the job. Be honest and be positive.

Presenting yourself well

Make sure you arrive for the interview in good time. Dress smartly and look business-like. Make sure, for example, that your hair is tidy and that your shoes are clean. Be confident, smile, and be polite. Listen carefully to what they ask you and answer clearly. Look the interviewer in the eye when you are talking to them.

left: *At your interviews make sure you present yourself as smartly as you can.*

Planning a career

Most people have several jobs in the course of their career. If you do well in a job, you may be **promoted**. Continued training helps you to progress. The more skills you acquire, the more opportunities open up. Things change fast, particularly in the world of IT. Look for opportunities and take advantage of them. Everyone's career path is different. The case study below shows one person's career. With determination, the sky's the limit!

CASE STUDY

Imran is a systems engineer and IT architect.

I graduated with a Maths degree and got into computers when they were still fairly new. I trained as a computer programmer with Lloyds Bank and, two years later, went to IBM. I switched to systems engineering and, after further training, I worked with IBM sales teams to make sure that the systems the customers bought worked well for them. I went on to become a database and data communications specialist helping customers, such as Safeway and Mars.

Several promotions later I became a systems engineering manager, dealing with people and businesses. I learnt a lot but found that I preferred the technical side – so I switched back and became an IT architect. This involved designing whole systems, called end-to-end design, and was something new. I was sent to Brussels for three years to teach IT architecture to people from IBM companies across Europe. This was the most satisfying job I've had – I really enjoyed teaching.

When I returned to London I continued as an IT architect, going to jobs all over the country, and then moved into computer security for the last four years of my time with IBM. The higher up the ladder you go, the more different skills you need – I was able to learn almost all my skills at IBM!

Further information

Careers websites

Please note that qualifications and courses are subject to change.

◎ City and Guilds (www.city-and-guilds.co.uk)
 – This website tells you all about City and Guilds qualifications.

◎ Connexions Direct (www.connexions-direct.com)
 – This website gives information and advice to young people, including learning and careers. It includes links to the Jobs4U careers database.

◎ Learndirect (www.learndirect-advice.co.uk)
 and Learndirect Scotland (www.learndirectscotland.com/)
 – Go to "Careers", then "Job profiles", and select "Administration" or "IT".

◎ Modern Apprenticeships, Scotland
 (www.scottish-enterprise.com/modernapprenticeships)
 – Check out the case studies of people already training.

◎ Need2Know: Learning (www.need2know.co.uk/learning)
 – This website gives information about studying and qualifications.

◎ Qualifications and Curriculum Authority (www.qca.org.uk/14-19)
 – Go to "Qualifications" and click on "Main qualification groups" to find out about NVQs.

◎ Scottish Vocational Qualifications (www.sqa.org.uk)
 – Find out all the latest qualifications information.

◎ The National Council for Work Experience
 (www.work-experience.org/)
 – Go to "Students and graduates" to search placements.

Magazines

Computer Weekly
– Read this for the latest IT news. It also includes lots of job advertisements.

.Net
– This monthly magazine covers the Internet.

Get ahead in IT and administration!

- ◎ Civil Service careers (www.careers.civil-service.gov.uk)
    - This UK Government site tells you about the work of the Civil Service and the kind of jobs available for different qualifications.
- ◎ Computer Clubs for Girls (www.cc4g.net)
    - This is a computer club designed for girls interested in IT, to help them develop their computer skills.
- ◎ Council for Administration (www.breakinto.biz)
    - This website tells you about administrative jobs for different levels of qualifications, from receptionist to managing director.
- ◎ e-skills UK (www.e-skills.com/training)
    - This website tells you what courses are available in your region in different IT skills.
- ◎ eskillspassport (www.e-skillspassport.com) – This website assesses which areas of IT you are strong in and which areas you need more training in. You have to pay to get your e-skills passport, but it is recognized by employers.
- ◎ Local Government Careers (www.lgcareers.com)
    - Go to this website to learn about local government, what it does, how it is run, and the careers they offer. It also gives tips on filling in application forms and interviews.

Books

Corfield, Rebecca. *Preparing Your Own CV* (Kogan Page, 2003)

Corfield, Rebecca. *Successful Interview Skills* (Kogan Page, 2006)

Faust, Bill and Michael. *Pitch Yourself* (Pearson Education, 2006)
– This book shows you how to write a CV that really sells *you*!

Fortune, Deborah. *Look Ahead Information Technology* (Heinemann Library, 2001)

Harris, Neil. *Getting into IT and the Internet* (Trotman, 2002)

accountant person who is responsible for keeping accurate financial records and who works out the profit a company or person has made

adapt change to fit a particular situation

agenda list of topics to be discussed at a meeting

analyst someone who studies a subject or situation and breaks it down into its different parts

application computer program designed for people to use and interact with

apprenticeship training scheme that allows you to work for money, learn, and become qualified at the same time.

assertive able to express yourself boldly and confidently

BTEC Business and Technician Education Council. The qualifications it awards include the HNC and HND (Higher National Certificate/Diploma).

Civil Service organization that runs the country in accordance with Government policy. It includes all branches of Government except elected politicians, the armed forces, and the law courts

clerical relating to routine office work

computer language code used to write instructions in a form that a computer can carry out. Computer languages include languages used to write computer programmes and languages used to markup documents for the Internet.

consultant person who has a lot of experience and provides expert professional advice

curriculum vitae/(CV) one or two sheets of paper with information about you, your skills, and your achievements

database collection of information that is arranged so that any piece of information can be easily found

dictation words that are spoken so that someone else can write or type them

fibre-optic transmitting information by sending light signals through very thin glass or plastic cables

grammatical obeying the rules of grammar

hardware machines and equipment used in computing work, such as computers, printers, scanners, CD roms, and printer cartridges

interactive reacting to each other. In IT, interactive means that the program and the user respond to each other.

logical using reason and thought to link one idea to another

marketing advertising and selling of goods or services, including special offers

methodical one step at a time, according to a system

meticulous paying attention to detail

minutes (of a meeting) written record of a meeting that includes the main points discussed and the decisions taken

multimedia combination of different ways of communicating information, including television, film, and print. In computers, multimedia is a combination of text, pictures, video, and sound.

network several interconnected computers

National Vocational Qualification/(NVQ) in England and Wales, a work-related, competence-based qualification that shows you have the knowledge and skills to do a job effectively. NVQs represent national standards that are recognized by employers throughout the UK.

petty cash small amount of money used to pay for minor office expenses

promote move up to a more responsible job

public company company whose shareholders are members of the public and whose shares are bought and sold on the Stock Exchange

public service service provided for the benefit of the public. Public services include the National Health Service, the police, Royal Mail, and train and bus services.

shorthand system of symbols or abbreviations used for writing quickly by hand

software programs that tell a computer what to do. Software includes applications such as computer games, music applications, and the programs that allow you to access the Internet. Software also includes the hidden programs that work "behind the scenes" in the computer to allow the computer to operate.

spreadsheet computer program that presents financial information in the form of a table. For example, a spreadsheet can be used to compare the profits made by selling different amounts of a product.

tactful discreetly taking account of other people's feelings

Index